J
636.213
B417
BELLVILLE, CHERYL
Round-up

MAR 1986

8.95

DATE DUE

14 May 86	21 Mar 8	MAY 1 2 1994
15 Aug 86	C2-1-90	AUG 1 9 1994
13 Mar 87	AUG 3 1 19	OCT 2 9 1994
24 Aug 87	C 12-11-90	MAY 2 7 1995
2 Oct 87	JAN 0 4 199	AUG 0 1 1995
20 Jan	MAR 1 8 19	DEC 2 6 1995
3 Feb 88	AUG 24 19	JUN 1 3 1996
17 Feb 88	DEC 2 0 19	NOV 1 6 1999
25 Mar 88	JUN 30 19	JUN 0 2 2000
6 Jul 88	C 5-13-93	JUN 2 7 20
10 Nov 88	SEP 1 1	JUL 0 6 20
2 Feb 89	C 1-13-9	

850892

**PARK COUNTY LIBRARY
SYSTEM
POWELL BRANCH LIBRARY**
Powell, Wyoming 82435

Round-up

Round-up

CHERYL WALSH BELLVILLE

850892

PARK COUNTY LIBRARY, POWELL, WYOMING

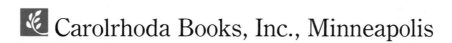

Carolrhoda Books, Inc., Minneapolis

The author would like to thank Lane and Midge Johnston for their continued help and support and particularly for their assistance in the preparation of this book. Thanks also to the Walkers and the Gruwells for allowing their round-ups to be photographed.

The photographs on pages 11, 15, 16, and 20 are used with permission from Charlton Photos, Milwaukee, Wisconsin.

Copyright © 1982 by Carolrhoda Books, Inc.

All rights reserved. International copyright secured.
No part of this book may be reproduced in any form whatsoever
without permission in writing from the publisher except for
the inclusion of brief quotations in an acknowledged review.

Manufactured in the United States of America

LIBRARY OF CONGRESS CATALOGING IN PUBLICATION DATA

Bellville, Cheryl Walsh.
  Round-up.

  Summary: Describes the activities that
take place at a spring cattle round-up.
    1. Ranch life—Juvenile literature.
  2. Cattle—Juvenile literature.   3.Beef
  cattle—Juvenile literature.   [1. Cattle.
  2. Ranch life]   I. Title.
  SF197.5.B44   636.2'13   81-18051
  ISBN 0-87614-187-4   AACR2

            1 2 3   4   5   6   7   8   9   10   88 87 86 85 84 83 82

to my mother and father

Spring round-up is the busiest and most exciting time of the year on a cattle ranch. Just about everyone who lives or works on the ranch, plus their friends and neighbors, will get involved. Depending on the size of the ranch, they will spend from one to several days rounding up, herding, and handling that ranch's cattle. Then the action will shift to a neighboring ranch, and so it will go until all of the calves in the area have been branded.

Throughout the winter and early spring, the herd has been kept in pastures near the ranch buildings so that the cattle can be fed hay and other supplements during the winter and so that the rancher can keep a careful watch on spring calving. If one of the cows is having difficulty calving, the rancher wants to be on hand to help out. Or if a young calf is in trouble, the rancher can carry it by horseback to the shelter of the buildings without too much difficulty. But even though they are relatively "close to home," the cattle can still be strewn over thousands of acres at round-up time.

Early in the morning on the first day of round-up, the riders catch their horses for the day, saddle up, and sometimes ride the bucks out of their mounts. The horses have had little work to do over the winter, and some of them haven't been ridden since the previous fall.

Horses are tremendously important to ranching. Every horse on a ranch must be comfortable with all aspects of working with cattle. Each horse must learn to stand quietly when a calf is taken aboard, watch and follow cattle, and anticipate their movements. A good cattle horse is strong, quiet, and responsive.

Horses and riders may have to travel long distances to round up all the cows and their calves. They will move the cattle along in ever-growing bunches as more cows and calves are found along the way.

When the cattle are near the corrals, the bunches are gathered together into a herd. The herd is kept together quietly for a while so that the cows and their calves can pair off (or "mother up"). When the cows and their calves have found each other, the rancher can tell which calf goes with which cow.

This is also the time to cut out any cattle that do not belong to the ranch. Representatives of the neighboring ranches are usually on hand to help. The neighbors' calves will be branded with the mark of the ranch that the mother carries.

In the days when most branding was done on the open range, cowboys on horseback had to surround the herd all day to keep the cattle together. If an animal broke away from the herd, a cowboy had to head it off and turn it back.

But today the cattle are moved into corrals after they have been checked and settled. There they are sprayed for protection from flies and cattle lice.

Now the cows and calves are separated, and the calves are penned together to await the battery of operations that will protect their health and identify them as part of the herd.

Today the only people on horseback during the actual branding are the ropers. A roper rides into the corral, ropes a calf around one or both hind legs, and pulls it to the branding fire.

18

At the fire the calf is thrown to the ground and held. In just a few minutes it will be branded, de-horned, ear-notched, castrated if it is a bull, and innoculated against diseases.

Branding is a method for identifying the calf as property of the ranch. A calf may be branded on its flank or on its shoulder or on its side, but all cattle in a herd are branded on the same spot. The brand itself is the personal mark of the ranch and is registered with the state brand board.

The branders are careful not to burn through the skin of the calf. They don't want to hurt the calf, but they do want to kill the hair follicles beneath the branding iron so that the brand will be obviously different from the rest of the calf's coat.

The calves' horns are removed so that they will not injure other de-horned (or "polled")
cattle or have an advantage over cattle without horns when competing for food.

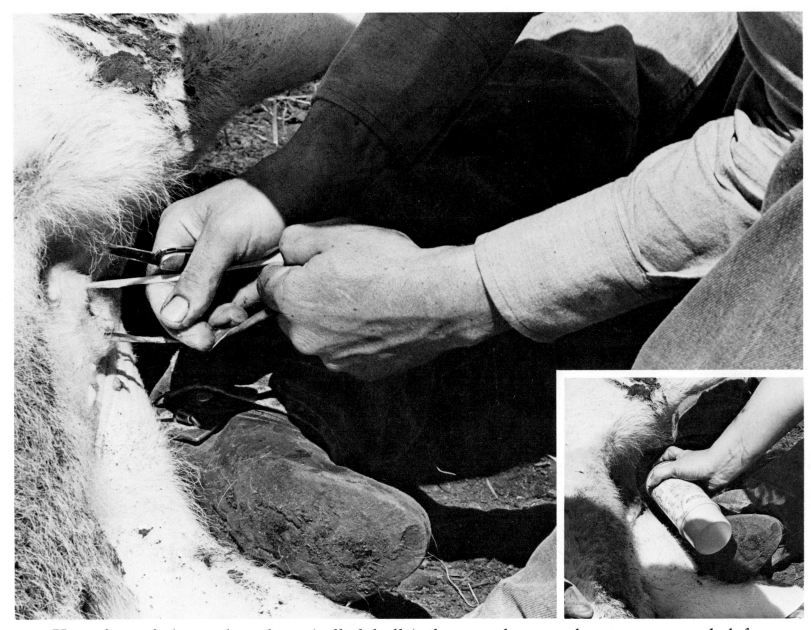

Very few of the male calves (called bulls) that are born each year are needed for breeding purposes, so most of the bull calves are castrated. This process will make them unable to reproduce when they become adults. Castrated bulls are called steers.

Ear-notching is done for identification during the winter months when the brand will be hidden by a thick coat. Ear-notching also makes it easy to identify a calf from a distance or from the front or side.

24

Finally the calves are innoculated against one or more of the cattle diseases most common in the area.

In a few minutes all of these procedures have been completed and the calf is released to the corral or to the waiting cow herd. The calves will be allowed to rest for a few days before they are moved to the summer grazing lands which may be several miles from the corrals.

At last all the calves are back with their mothers.

The horses have been fed and watered.

It's time to relax and have dinner. While the work was going on in the corrals, dinner was being prepared and brought to the location in chuckwagon style. These days dinner is spread on the tailgates of pick-up trucks, but the food is the traditional fare — beef with home-made trimmings. Everyone fills a plate and sits down to talk over the day's work.

850892